Grade 3

Skill Practice

T E A C H I N G   G U I D E

	DATE DUE		

Developmental Studies Center
2000 Embarcadero, Suite 305
Oakland, CA 94606-5300
(800) 666-7270, fax: (510) 464-3670
www.devstu.org

ISBN-13: 978-1-59892-318-6
ISBN-10: 1-59892-318-8

Printed in the United States of America

1 2 3 4 5 6 7 8 9 10 MLY 11 10 09 08 07

Table of Contents

continues

Table of Contents *continued*

Introduction

Welcome to the *Being a Writer Skill Practice Teaching Guide.* This component, along with the *Student Skill Practice Book,* supplements the *Being a Writer* core program by providing additional activities to help students practice the skills and conventions of written English. The skills selected for inclusion in this book are developmentally appropriate and consistent with prevailing standards of writing instruction at grade 3.

How to Use These Mini-lessons

You can use these 10- to 15-minute mini-lessons at any time to teach or review grammar, usage, punctuation, and capitalization skills with your class. Mini-lessons can reinforce skills taught in the core program, or they can teach or review additional skills required by your district or taught in prior years. The table on the following page shows which skills are included in these mini-lessons, if and where they are taught in the core program at this grade (marked as "Taught"), and which units in the core program lend themselves to continued practice of those skills (marked with an "X").

To teach these mini-lessons, you will need an overhead projector, transparencies of the blackline masters (see pages 37–54), extra blank transparencies, and overhead pens. Some mini-lessons also include steps that require chart paper. The students may need separate sheets of paper to complete some of the activities.

While mastery of grammatical terms is not a primary goal of this program, it is helpful for students to hear these terms regularly when learning English language conventions. We encourage you to use proper grammatical terminology when discussing parts of speech and other conventions with your students.

Grade 3 Skills

Taught = taught directly in the unit　　**X** = appropriate to practice

Grammar and Usage	Personal Narrative	Fiction	Expository Nonfiction	Functional Nonfiction	Revisiting the Writing Community
Recognize and use nouns	X	X	X	X	X
Recognize and use adjectives	X	X	X	X	X
Recognize and use verbs		**Taught**	X	X	X
Recognize and use contractions	X	X	X	X	X
Recognize and correct incomplete sentences		**Taught**	**Taught**	X	X
Use singular and plural forms of regular and irregular nouns	X	X	X	X	X
Use past, present, and future verb tenses	X	X			X
Demonstrate understanding of subject-verb agreement	X	X	X	X	X
Demonstrate understanding of noun-pronoun agreement	X	X	X	X	X
Use comparative and superlative adjectives	X	X	X	X	X

Punctuation and Capitalization	Personal Narrative	Fiction	Expository Nonfiction	Functional Nonfiction	Revisiting the Writing Community
Use commas in dates and greetings/closings of letters	X	X	X	X	X
Use commas in a series			**Taught**	X	X
Use quotation marks to punctuate speech		**Taught**	X	X	X
Use apostrophes to show possession			**Taught**	X	X
Capitalize proper nouns including holidays and special events	X	X	X	X	X
Arrange words in alphabetical order	X	X	X	X	X

Skill Practice
Mini-lessons

Grammar and Usage

Skill: Recognize and use nouns

Materials: Transparency of "An Acrobatic Ape" (page 38)
Overhead pen

Lesson:

1. Explain that the students will practice recognizing and using nouns to help them in their writing. Explain that *nouns* are words in the English language that stand for people (or animals), places, or things (including plants).

2. Show part A of "An Acrobatic Ape" on the overhead projector and read it aloud.

3. Reread the first sentence. Point out that the noun *gibbon* has been underlined. Ask:

    Q *What other nouns do you see in this passage? Is this noun a person (or animal), place, or thing?*

    As the students respond, underline the nouns on the transparency. (See "An Acrobatic Ape: Corrections" on the facing page.)

4. Brainstorm three lists of nouns (for people/animals, places, and things) as a class and record them on a chart labeled "Interesting Nouns." (Post the chart, add to it over time, and encourage the students to use the nouns in their own writing.)

5. Read part B aloud. Choose one word from each list on the chart and write a short passage using the three words. Underline the words and any other nouns in the passage.

6. (Optional) Ask the students to open to *Student Skill Practice Book* page 1. Read the directions aloud and have the students work individually or in pairs on the activity. For additional practice with this skill, assign the activities on pages 2–4 of the *Student Skill Practice Book*. (For corrections for these activities, see pages 56–57 of the *Skill Practice Teaching Guide*.)

An Acrobatic Ape: Corrections

A.   **Nouns are underlined in the passage below.**

A <u>gibbon</u> is a small <u>ape</u> from <u>Asia</u>. It lives in the <u>forest</u>. It has long <u>arms</u> and no <u>tail</u>. It can grasp and carry <u>things</u> with its <u>hands</u> and <u>feet</u>.

<u>Gibbons</u> live in <u>families</u>, with a <u>mother</u>, a <u>father</u>, and <u>offspring</u> (<u>children</u>). They eat mostly <u>fruit</u>. They eat other <u>things</u>, too, including <u>flowers</u>, <u>leaves</u>, <u>insects</u>, <u>spiders</u>, and <u>birds</u>. They do not build <u>nests</u> like other <u>apes</u>. Instead, they sleep sitting up between <u>branches</u>. They use their <u>arms</u> to swing from <u>tree</u> to <u>tree</u>. They can also leap between <u>trees</u>. They are so quick and graceful that almost no <u>predator</u> can catch them.

B.   **Check for the appropriate use of nouns in the passage.**

Grammar and Usage

Skill: Recognize and use adjectives

Materials: Transparency of "The Haunted House" (page 39)
Overhead pen

Lesson:

1. Explain that the students will practice recognizing and using adjectives to help them in their writing. Explain that *adjectives* are words in the English language that describe nouns.

2. Show part A of "The Haunted House" on the overhead projector and read it aloud.

3. Reread the first sentence. Point out that the adjective *haunted* has been underlined. Ask:

   Q *What other adjectives do you see in this passage?*

   As the students respond, underline the adjectives on the transparency. (See "The Haunted House: Corrections" on the facing page.)

4. Think aloud and model adding an adjective to the passage (such as the word *squeaky* before *door*); then ask:

   Q *What other adjectives could we add to this passage?*

   Use the students' suggestions to add a few adjectives to the passage.

5. Brainstorm a list of adjectives as a class and record them on a chart labeled "Interesting Adjectives." (Post the chart, add to it over time, and encourage the students to use the adjectives in their own writing.)

6. Read part B aloud. Use the students' suggestions from the chart to write a short passage that includes interesting adjectives. Underline the adjectives.

7. (Optional) Ask the students to open to *Student Skill Practice Book* page 5. Read the directions aloud and have the students work individually or in pairs on the activity. For additional practice with this skill, assign the activities on pages 6–8 of the *Student Skill Practice Book*. (For corrections for these activities, see pages 58–59 of the *Skill Practice Teaching Guide*.)

The Haunted House: Corrections

A.   **Adjectives are underlined, and examples of additional adjectives are given.**

No one has lived in the <u>haunted</u> house for <u>many</u> years. It sits

behind an <u>old</u>, <u>white</u> fence with a <u>broken</u>_, creaking_ gate at the top of a_ _high_ hill.

Only <u>brave</u> children dare to tiptoe through the <u>weed-filled</u> yard,

up the <u>cracked</u> steps, and onto the <u>sagging</u> porch. <u>Braver</u> children

peer through the_ _cobwebbed_ windows. The <u>bravest</u> children open the_ _squeaky_ door

and step into the <u>dark</u> hall. When they do, they're sure to hear a

sound that chills their bones, the sound of a_ _shrill_ voice singing a_ _scary_ song.

B.   **Check for the appropriate use of adjectives in the passage.**

Grammar and Usage

Skill: Recognize and use verbs

Materials: Transparency of "How to Make S'mores" (page 40)
               Overhead pen

Lesson:

1. Explain that the students will practice recognizing and using verbs to help them in their writing. Explain that *verbs* are action words in the English language.

2. Show part A of "How to Make S'mores" on the overhead projector and read it aloud.

3. Reread the first sentence. Point out that the verb *to prepare* has been underlined. Ask:

    Q *What other verbs do you see in this passage?*

    As the students respond, underline the verbs. (See "How to Make S'mores: Corrections" on the facing page.)

4. Read part B aloud. Use the students' suggestions to write a short "how to" passage that includes interesting verbs. Underline the verbs.

5. (Optional) Brainstorm verbs as a class and record them on a chart labeled "Interesting Verbs." Post the chart and add to it over time. Encourage the students to use the verbs in their own writing.

6. (Optional) Ask the students to open to *Student Skill Practice Book* page 9. Read the directions aloud and have the students work individually or in pairs on the activity. For additional practice with this skill, assign the activities on pages 10–12 of the *Student Skill Practice Book*. (For corrections for these activities, see pages 60–61 of the *Skill Practice Teaching Guide*.)

How to Make S'mores: Corrections

A.   **Verbs are underlined in the passage below.**

To prepare s'mores, you will need a campfire, a stick,
marshmallows, graham crackers, and a chocolate bar. Poke
the stick through a marshmallow. With an adult nearby, hold
the stick over the campfire. Toast the marshmallow until it is
golden brown. Remove the marshmallow from the stick and
smash it down on a graham cracker. Place a piece of chocolate
on top of the marshmallow. Put another graham cracker
on top. Enjoy your s'more—and then make some more!

B.   **Check for the appropriate use of verbs in the passage.**

Grammar and Usage

Skill: Recognize and use contractions

Materials: Transparency of "Mountains of Sand" (page 41)
Overhead pen

Lesson:

1. Show part A of "Mountains of Sand" on the overhead projector and read it aloud. Read the words *are not*. Explain that putting two words together and replacing one or more of the letters with an apostrophe makes a shorter word called a *contraction*. Write the word *aren't* beneath *are not*. Explain that *aren't* is a contraction of *are not* and that the apostrophe takes the place of the *o*. Read the remaining examples in part A and ask the students to help you make a contraction out of each set of words.

2. Read part B aloud. Read the contraction *shouldn't*. Ask:

   Q *What two words make this contraction? What letter(s) does the apostrophe replace?*

   As the students respond, write down the words that make the contraction. Repeat with the remaining examples in part B.

4. Read part C aloud; then reread the first sentence. Point out that the contraction *I'm* has been underlined and the words *I am* have been written above it. Ask:

   Q *What is another contraction you see in the passage? What are the two words that make that contraction?*

   As the students respond, underline the contractions and write the words that make the contractions above them. (See "Mountains of Sand: Corrections" on the facing page.)

5. (Optional) Brainstorm a list of contractions as a class and record them on a chart labeled "Contractions." Post the chart and add to it over time.

6. (Optional) Use the students' suggestions to write a short passage using contractions.

7. (Optional) Ask the students to open to *Student Skill Practice Book* page 13. Read the directions aloud and have the students work individually or in pairs on the activity. For additional practice with this skill, assign the activities on pages 14–16 of the *Student Skill Practice Book*. (For corrections for these activities, see pages 62–63 of the *Skill Practice Teaching Guide*.)

Mountains of Sand: Corrections

A. **Answers are shown below.**

are not	he will	I am	they are
aren't	he'll	I'm	they're

B. **Answers are shown below.**

shouldn't	I'll	it's	she's
should not	I will	it is	she is

C. **Contractions are underlined. The words that make each contraction are written above it.**

I am
I'm getting ready to go on a trip. My mom said to pack light

is not   *do not*
because she isn't going to carry my bag for me. I don't want

We are
to forget anything. We're going to visit some sand dunes in

I have   *they are*
Colorado. From what I've heard, they're giant mountains of sand.

he is   *does not*
My dad said he's going to ski down the dunes. I hope he doesn't

cannot   *he will*
hurt himself. I can't ski, but I think he'll let me sled down instead.

did not   *it is*
I didn't know that it's possible to ski and sled on sand.

Grammar and Usage

Skill: Recognize and correct incomplete sentences

Materials: Transparency of "How the Platypus Got Its Nose" (page 42)
              Overhead pen

Lesson:

1. Show part A of "How the Platypus Got Its Nose" on the overhead projector and read it
    aloud without the correction. Ask:

    Q *What do you notice about this paragraph?*

    Point out that some of the sentences are *incomplete*.

2. Point out that the second sentence is incomplete and read the sentence with the
    correction. Continue reading the passage one sentence at a time. For each sentence, ask:

    Q *Who or what is this sentence about? What is [the platypus] doing?*

    Explain that if both questions cannot be answered, the sentence is incomplete.
    Underline each incomplete sentence and ask:

    Q *What can we add to this sentence to make it complete?*

    Use carets to insert the students' suggestions into the text to complete the sentences.
    (See "How the Platypus Got Its Nose: Corrections" on the facing page.)

3. Read part B aloud. Use the students' suggestions to write a short passage
    incorporating the starter sentence. As you write, make sure the students are
    suggesting complete sentences.

4. (Optional) Ask the students to open to *Student Skill Practice Book* page 17. Read the
    directions aloud and have the students work individually or in pairs on the activity. For
    additional practice with this skill, assign the activities on pages 18–20 of the *Student Skill
    Practice Book*. (For corrections for these activities, see pages 64–65 of the *Skill Practice
    Teaching Guide*.)

How the Platypus Got Its Nose: Corrections

A.   **Incomplete sentences are underlined. Inserted text will vary. Examples are shown below.**

One day a platypus was walking along the riverbed, minding
his own business. His long, round nose *sniffed at the ground Suddenly a kangaroo* hopped right on his nose.
The startled platypus *looked up in shock* Perhaps that is how the platypus got a nose

like a duck's bill.

B.   **Check for the use of complete sentences in the passage.**

Grammar and Usage

Skill: Use singular and plural forms of regular and irregular nouns

Materials: Transparency of "A Visit to the Museum" (page 43)
Overhead pen

Lesson:

1. Show part A of "A Visit to the Museum" on the overhead projector and read it aloud. Explain that a noun can be *singular* (one person/animal, place, or thing) or *plural* (more than one person/animal, place, or thing).

2. Read the example (*student/students*) and explain that to make many nouns plural, all you have to do is add an *s*. Ask:

   Q *What other nouns do you see in the picture? How can we make [bone] plural?*

   As the students respond, write the singular and plural nouns in the blanks on the transparency. When the opportunity arises, explain when you would add *es* (words ending in *s*, *x*, *sh*, or *ch*), change *y* to *i* and add *es*, change the spelling, or make no change to make plural nouns. (See "A Visit to the Museum: Corrections" on the facing page.)

4. Read part B aloud. Use the students' suggestions to write a short passage using plural nouns. Underline the plural nouns in the passage.

5. (Optional) Ask the students to open to *Student Skill Practice Book* page 21. Read the directions aloud and have the students work individually or in pairs on the activity. For additional practice with this skill, assign the activities on pages 22–24 of the *Student Skill Practice Book*. (For corrections for these activities, see pages 66–67 of the *Skill Practice Teaching Guide*.)

A Visit to the Museum: Corrections

A. **Answers may vary.**

	Singular	*Plural*
1.	student	students
2.	bone	bones
3.	starfish	starfish
4.	tooth	teeth
5.	claw	claws
6.	shell	shells
7.	skeleton	skeletons

B. **Check for the appropriate use of plural nouns in the passage.**

Grammar and Usage

Skill: Use past, present, and future verb tenses

Materials: Transparency of "What I Want to Be" (page 44)
Overhead pen

Lesson:

1. Show part A of "What I Want to Be" on the overhead projector and read the directions and first paragraph aloud. Ask:

   Q *When is this paragraph happening?*

   Explain that the first paragraph happened when the writer was little and is written mostly in the *past tense.*

   Repeat this procedure with the second and third paragraphs, explaining that they are written in *present* and *future tenses*, respectively.

2. Explain that you can tell the tense of a passage by reading the verbs. Reread the first sentence. Point out that the word *was* is a verb in the past tense; it has been underlined and marked *pa* for past tense. Ask:

   Q *What other verbs do you see in the first paragraph? What tense is that verb?*

   As the students respond, underline the verbs and write the tense above each one. Repeat this procedure for the second and third paragraphs. (See "What I Want to Be: Corrections" on the facing page.)

3. Read part B aloud. Use the students' suggestions to write three short paragraphs using past, present, and future verb tenses. Underline the verbs.

4. (Optional) Brainstorm verbs as a class and record the past, present, and future tenses of each on a chart labeled "Past, Present, and Future Verb Tenses." Post the chart and add to it over time. Encourage the students to use the verb tenses in their own writing.

6. (Optional) Ask the students to open to *Student Skill Practice Book* page 25. Read the directions aloud and have the students work individually or in pairs on the activity. For additional practice with this skill, assign the activities on pages 26–28 of the *Student Skill Practice Book*. (For corrections for these activities, see pages 68–69 of the *Skill Practice Teaching Guide*.)

What I Want to Be: Corrections

A.   **Verbs are underlined and marked to signify past (*pa*), present (*pr*), or future (*f*) tense.**

When I *was* little, I *said*, "I *will be* a veterinarian someday."
I *read* books about vets. I *asked* my dog's vet questions about
her work.

Now I *tell* everyone, "I *will be* a writer." I *read* the "About
the Author" sections in books. I *carry* a notepad and *jot* down
my ideas as they *pop* into my head. I *write* stories and poems and
show them to my family.

Later on, though, maybe I *will decide* that I *will be* something
else entirely. Maybe I *will consider* a career as a firefighter or
forest ranger. Maybe I *will have* more than one career. That way
I *will fulfill* at least a few of my dreams.

B.   **Check for the appropriate use of past, present, and future verb tenses in the three paragraphs.**

Grammar and Usage

Skill: Demonstrate understanding of subject-verb agreement

Materials: Transparency of "My Sister the Space Alien" (page 45)
Overhead pen

Lesson:

1. Show part A of "My Sister the Space Alien" on the overhead projector and read it aloud. Ask:

   Q *What do you notice?*

   Point out that the passage sounds strange because *the subjects and verbs don't agree.*

2. Reread the first sentence and point out that the incorrect verb is underlined and the correct verb is written above it. Read the next sentence and model underlining the incorrect verb and writing the correct verb above it. Ask:

   Q *What other verbs are incorrect? How can we correct them?*

   As the students respond, underline and correct the other verbs in the passage. (See "My Sister the Space Alien: Corrections" on the facing page.)

4. Read part B aloud. Read the first pair of verbs and the sample sentences aloud. Explain that *play* agrees with *I* and *plays* agrees with *he.*

5. Ask:

   Q *What is a sentence we could write using the verb* is*? What is a sentence we could write using the verb* are*?*

   Use the students' suggestions to complete the remaining sentences.

6. (Optional) Ask the students to open to *Student Skill Practice Book* page 29. Read the directions aloud and have the students work individually or in pairs on the activity. For additional practice with this skill, assign the activities on pages 30–32 of the *Student Skill Practice Book.* (For corrections for these activities, see pages 70–71 of the *Skill Practice Teaching Guide.*)

My Sister the Space Alien: Corrections

A. **Incorrect verbs are underlined, and the correct verbs are written above.**

                              pretends   *moves*

Sometimes my sister <u>pretend</u> to be from outer space. She <u>move</u>

                             invents

her arms and legs stiffly, like a robot. She <u>invent</u> strange words

                         laugh

like "oogle-boogle." My brother and I <u>laughs</u>. When my parents

say

<u>says</u>, "Time for bed," my sister just <u>say</u>, "Munka-munka-munka."

           tell   *says*

                             responds

When they <u>tells</u> her, "Clean your room," she <u>respond</u>, "Frzzz-

           stand   *scratch*

frzzz-frzzz." They <u>stands</u> there and <u>scratches</u> their heads. They

do

<u>does</u> not understand space alien language.

B. **Check for subject-verb agreement in the sentences.**

Grammar and Usage

Skill: Demonstrate understanding of noun-pronoun agreement

Materials: Transparency of "We Love Our Pet" (page 46)
              Overhead pen

Lesson:

1. Explain that the students will practice using *pronouns* correctly to help them in their writing. Explain that pronouns are words that stand for nouns, such as *he, she, it, we*, and *they*.

2. Show part A of "We Love Our Pet" on the overhead projector and read the first set of sentences aloud. Explain that the pronouns *her*, *she*, and *hers* are used to replace the name *Jaya*. Read the second set of sentences aloud and ask:

   Q *What words can we use to replace* [Benjy] *in these sentences?*

   As the students respond, write the pronouns in the blanks on the transparency. Continue to replace the names in bold to complete all four sets of sentences. (See "We Love Our Pet: Corrections" on the facing page.)

4. Read the directions for part B aloud. Use the students' suggestions to write more sentences about Max, the pet mouse.

5. (Optional) Use the students' suggestions to write a short passage using pronouns. Underline the pronouns used in the passage.

6. (Optional) Ask the students to open to *Student Skill Practice Book* page 33. Read the directions aloud and have the students work individually or in pairs on the activity. For additional practice with this skill, assign the activities on pages 34–36 of the *Student Skill Practice Book*. (For corrections for these activities, see pages 72–73 of the *Skill Practice Teaching Guide*.)

We Love Our Pet: Corrections

A.   **The correct pronouns are shown below.**

1.   **Jaya** loves Max, ____her____ pet mouse. Max loves ____her____.

   ____She____ is glad that Max is ____hers____.

2.   **Benjy** loves Max, ____his____ pet mouse. Max loves ____him____.

   ____He____ is glad that Max is ____his____.

3.   **Lee and Lisa** love Max, ____their____ pet mouse. Max loves

   ____them____. ____They____ are glad that Max is ____theirs____.

4.   **My family** loves Max, ____our____ pet mouse. Max loves

   ____us____. ____We____ are glad that Max is ____ours____.

B.   **Revised sentences are shown below. The second sentences will vary.**

1.   **Max** likes to eat **mushrooms**.

   He likes to eat them. They taste good.

2.   **Max and I** play with **marbles**.

   We play with them. They are fun.

Grammar and Usage

Skill: Use comparative and superlative adjectives

Materials: Transparency of "Fast and Heavy" (page 47)
Overhead pen

Lesson:

1. Have three students with different lengths of hair come to the front of the room. Demonstrate the use of *comparative and superlative adjectives* using the adjective *short* or *long*. You might say, "[Marcos] has *short* hair. [Marcos] has *shorter* hair than [Lydia]. [Marcos] has the *shortest* hair of all three students." Write the endings *er* and *est* where everyone can see them and explain that these endings can be added to adjectives when making comparisons.

2. Show part A of "Fast and Faster" on the overhead projector and read it aloud. Point to the third sentence in #1 and reread it aloud; then ask:

   Q *What ending do we need to add to the word* fast *to complete this sentence?*

   As the students respond, fill in the blank and complete the sentence. Repeat with the remaining sets of sentences. (See "Fast and Heavy: Corrections" on the facing page.)

3. Read part B aloud. Use the students' suggestions to write a short passage that includes comparative and superlative adjectives.

4. (Optional) Ask the students to open to *Student Skill Practice Book* page 37. Read the directions aloud and have the students work individually or in pairs on the activity. For additional practice with this skill, assign the activities on pages 38–40 of the *Student Skill Practice Book*. (For corrections for these activities, see pages 74–75 of the *Skill Practice Teaching Guide*.)

Fast and Heavy: Corrections

A. **Corrections are given below.**

1. The giraffe is **fast**.

   The coyote is ___faster___ than the giraffe.

   The cheetah is the ___fastest___ of them all.

2. The coyote is **heavy**.

   The cheetah is ___heavier___ than the coyote.

   The giraffe is the ___heaviest___ of them all.

B. **Check for the appropriate use of comparative and superlative adjectives in the passage.**

Punctuation and Capitalization

Skill: Use commas in dates and greetings/closings of letters

Materials: Transparency of "The Letters of Sun and Moon" (page 48)
Overhead pen

Lesson:

1. Explain that the students will practice using commas in dates and in the greetings and closings of letters to help them in their writing. Explain that a *greeting* is the way someone says hello in a letter, and that a *closing* is the way someone says goodbye in a letter.

2. Show part A of "The Letters of Sun and Moon" on the overhead projector and read it aloud. Point out that the date of the letter is indented to the far right, and that the greeting ("Dear Moon") is on the left-hand side below the date. The closing ("Sincerely") is below the last line and is also indented to the far right. Circle the commas in the date, greeting, and closing. Ask:

   Q *What do you notice about how commas are used in this letter?*

3. Read Part B of "The Letters of Sun and Moon" aloud. Ask:

   Q *Where do we need to add commas?*

   As the students respond, insert commas on the transparency. (See "The Letters of Sun and Moon: Corrections" on the facing page.)

4. Read part C aloud. Use the students' suggestions to write a continued exchange between Sun and Moon, or using two new correspondents. Model using commas in the date, greeting, and closing of each letter.

5. (Optional) Have the students each write a letter to a member of the class, a friend, or a family member. Remind them to use commas in the date, greeting, and closing.

6. (Optional) Ask the students to open to *Student Skill Practice Book* page 41. Read the directions aloud and have the students work individually or in pairs on the activity. For additional practice with this skill, assign the activities on pages 42–44 of the *Student Skill Practice Book*. (For corrections for these activities, see pages 76–77 of the *Skill Practice Teaching Guide*.)

The Letters of Sun and Moon: Corrections

A.   Commas are circled in the date, greeting, and closing.

January 31, 2010

Dear Moon,

   I miss you. I try to stay up until you arrive each evening. Most

of the time, though, you don't show up till past my bedtime.

Sincerely,

Sun

B.   Correct use of commas is shown below.

February 17, 2010

Dear Sun,

   I miss you, too. It does get chilly up here without you. But I

do love the peace, quiet, and darkness of nighttime, when almost

everyone's asleep.

Your friend,

Moon

**C.   Check for the appropriate use of commas in the dates, greetings, and closings
of the written letters.**

Punctuation and Capitalization

Skill: Use commas in a series

Materials: Transparency of "A Cooperative Cactus" (page 49)
Overhead pen

Lesson:

1. Show part A of "A Cooperative Cactus" on the overhead projector and read it aloud. Ask:

   Q *What do you notice about how commas are used in this passage?*

   Explain that in a *series*, or list, of three or more things in a sentence, commas are used to separate each item in the series. The word *and* or *or* is used after the final comma and before the last item.

2. Read part B aloud; then ask:

   Q *Where do you see a series in this passage? Where in that series should we add comma?*

   As the students respond, add commas on the transparency. (See "A Cooperative Cactus: Corrections" on the facing page.)

3. Read part C aloud. Use the students' suggestions to write a couple of sentences with series in them. (Possible topics include favorite foods and after-school routines.) Ask the students to tell you where you need to add commas in each series.

4. (Optional) Ask the students to open to *Student Skill Practice Book* page 45. Read the directions aloud and have the students work individually or in pairs on the activity. For additional practice with this skill, assign the activities on pages 46–48 of the *Student Skill Practice Book*. (For corrections for these activities, see pages 78–79 of the *Skill Practice Teaching Guide*.)

A Cooperative Cactus: Corrections

B.   Correct use of commas is shown below.

Coyotes, foxes, squirrels, and other animals eat its red fruit and tiny, black seeds. They sit in its shade to cool off. Gila woodpeckers peck holes in its sides to live in. These "hotel rooms" are used by other animals such as insects, bats, and rats when the woodpeckers move out. Humans use the long, straight rods inside the saguaro to make roofs, fences, and fuel.

C.   Check for the appropriate use of commas in a series in the sentences.

Punctuation and Capitalization

Skill: Use quotation marks to punctuate speech

Materials: Transparency of "The Bad Joke" (page 50)
Overhead pen

Lesson:

1. Explain that the students will practice using *quotation marks* to help them show when someone is speaking in their writing.

2. Show part A of "The Bad Joke" on the overhead projector and read it aloud. Reread the first sentence aloud; then ask:

   Q *Who is speaking in this sentence? What words does she say?*

   Point out that quotation marks surround the words Kim has said. Remind the students that the words *asked Kim* tell the reader who is speaking; these words are part of the sentence but are not part of what she is saying, so they are not included inside the quotation marks. Ask:

   Q *Where else are quotation marks needed in this story?*

   As the students respond, add quotation marks to the remaining sentences. (See "The Bad Joke: Corrections" on the facing page.)

3. Read part B aloud. Use the students' suggestions to write a continuation of the dialogue between Kim and Nico. Invite the students to tell you where to insert quotation marks in the dialogue.

5. (Optional) Ask the students to open to *Student Skill Practice Book* page 49. Read the directions aloud and have the students work individually or in pairs on the activity. For additional practice with this skill, assign the activities on pages 50–52 of the *Student Skill Practice Book*. (For corrections for these activities, see pages 80–81 of the *Skill Practice Teaching Guide*.)

Skill Practice Mini-lesson

The Bad Joke: Corrections

A. **Correct use of quotation marks is shown below.**

"Nico, do you want to hear a joke?" asked Kim.

"Sure," said Nico.

"What should you do to a blue elephant?" asked Kim.

"I don't know," Nico replied. "What should you do to a blue

elephant?"

Kim answered, "You should try to cheer him up."

"That is a really bad joke," said Nico.

"It is not bad. It is funny!" exclaimed Kim.

"If you want to hear a funny joke, I'll tell you one," said Nico.

B. **Check for the appropriate use of quotation marks in the written dialogue.**

Punctuation and Capitalization

Skill: Use apostrophes to show possession

Materials: Transparency of "Randy's Burgers" (page 51)
Overhead pen

Lesson:

1. Explain that the students will practice using *apostrophes* to show that something belongs to someone or something else.

2. Show part A of "Randy's Burgers" on the overhead projector and read it aloud. Reread the first two sentences. Note that the word *Randy's* is underlined and explain that the *'s* at the end of *Randy* lets the reader know that the restaurant belongs to Randy. Ask:

   Q *What words in the next sentence show that something belongs to someone or something else? Who does the thing belong to? What is the thing that belongs to the [waiters]?*

   As the students respond, underline the words that show possession on the transparency. When you encounter the phrase *waiters' trays*, explain that there is more than one waiter, but the phrase *waiters's trays* would be awkward to read. In cases like this when the noun is plural, the second *s* is dropped, leaving only the apostrophe. (See "Randy's Burgers: Corrections" on the facing page.)

   Continue the procedure for the remaining sentences.

3. Read part B aloud. Point out that in the example one word is used from each column to create a sentence, and *'s* is added to *Rhonda* to show that the hamburger belongs to her. Use the students' suggestions to write additional sentences.

4. (Optional) Ask the students to open to *Student Skill Practice Book* page 53. Read the directions aloud and have the students work individually or in pairs on the activity. For additional practice with this skill, assign the activities on pages 54–56 of the *Student Skill Practice Book*. (For corrections for these activities, see pages 82–83 of the *Skill Practice Teaching Guide*.)

Randy's Burgers: Corrections

A. **Words that use apostrophes to show possession are underlined below.**

<u>Randy's</u> Restaurant is famous for its hamburgers. The <u>waiters'</u> trays are even shaped like burgers. The <u>restaurant's</u> specialty is the Randy Burger. It is a giant hamburger with lettuce, tomato, cheese, and pickles. Randy picks the vegetables from his <u>neighbor's</u> garden. He uses his <u>family's</u> secret recipe to make the hamburger patties.

B. **Sentences will vary. Check for the correct use of apostrophes.**

1. <u>Rhonda's hamburger is delicious.</u>

2. <u>Randy's shakes are thick.</u>

3. <u>The customers' stomachs are full.</u>

Punctuation and Capitalization

Skill: Capitalize proper nouns including holidays and special events

Materials: Transparency of "The Boston Marathon" (page 52)
Overhead pen

Lesson:

1. Explain that the students will practice *capitalizing proper nouns* to help them in their writing. Tell the students that a proper noun names a specific person, place, or thing and begins with a capital letter.

2. Show part A of "The Boston Marathon" on the overhead projector and read it aloud. Point out that *Boston Marathon* is underlined. Explain that *Boston Marathon* is the name of a special event so it needs to be capitalized. Ask:

   Q *What other proper nouns do you see in this sentence?*

   As the students respond, underline the proper nouns. Continue to identify and underline the proper nouns in the rest of the passage. (See "The Boston Marathon: Corrections" on the facing page.)

3. Read part B aloud. Review the underlined words in the first sentence; then ask:

   Q *What kind of proper noun is [Patriot's Day]? What does [Patriot's Day] name?*

   As students respond, write the different types of proper nouns in a list. Continue to do this for the rest of the sentences in the passage.

4. Read part C aloud. Use the students' suggestions to list proper nouns that fit in the selected categories.

5. (Optional) Ask the students to open to *Student Skill Practice Book* page 57. Read the directions aloud and have the students work individually or in pairs on the activity. For additional practice with this skill, assign the activities on pages 58–60 of the *Student Skill Practice Book*. (For corrections for these activities, see pages 84–85 of the *Skill Practice Teaching Guide*.)

The Boston Marathon: Corrections

A.   **Proper nouns are underlined.**

The <u>Boston Marathon</u> is held every <u>Patriot's Day</u> in <u>Boston</u>, <u>Massachusetts</u>. The first <u>Boston Marathon</u> was run on <u>Monday</u>, <u>April</u> 19, 1897. There were 15 runners at the start, and 10 finished. Now, thousands of runners come from all over the world to compete in the race. In 2007, one runner competed from space! Astronaut <u>Sunita Williams</u> ran the marathon while in orbit on the <u>International Space Station</u>. She circled the <u>Earth</u> at least twice while running the 26.2 miles on a treadmill.

B.   **Types of proper nouns in the passage are shown below.**

- special events
- days of the week
- names of people
- holidays
- names of places

- names of planets
- names of cities
- names of months
- names of states

C.   **Check for appropriate examples of proper nouns.**

Punctuation and Capitalization

Skill: Arrange words in alphabetical order

Materials: Transparency of "A Place for Everything" (page 53)
                 Overhead pen

Lesson:

1. Show part A of "A Place for Everything" on the overhead projector and read it aloud. Model identifying the word that would come first alphabetically. Point out that both *queen* and *quart* start with the same two letters so you will have to look at the next letter to find out which one will come first. Write *quart* on the first line; then ask:

    Q *Which word will come next?*

    As the students respond, write the words in the appropriate order. Continue until all the blanks are filled; then have the students check whether the answer to the riddle makes sense. (See "A Place for Everything: Corrections" on the facing page.)

2. Read part B aloud. Use the students' suggestions to fill in the blanks.

3. (Optional) Ask the students to open to *Student Skill Practice Book* page 61. Read the directions aloud and have the students work individually or in pairs on the activity. For additional practice with this skill, assign the activities on pages 62–64 of the *Student Skill Practice Book*. (For corrections for these activities, see pages 86–87 of the *Skill Practice Teaching Guide*.)

A Place for Everything: Corrections

A.   The alphabetized list and riddle answer are given below.

queen   **1.**   __q__   __u__   [__ə__]   __r__   __t__

quart   **2.**   [__q__]   __u__   __e__   __e__   __n__

sting   **3.**   __q__   [__u__]   __i__   __e__   __t__

quiet   **4.**   __s__   [__i__]   __g__   __h__   __t__

silly   **5.**   __s__   __i__   __l__   [__l__]   __y__

sight   **6.**   __s__   [__t__]   __i__   __n__   __g__

What do you call a porcupine wrapped in a blanket?

__ə__   __q__   __u__   __i__   __l__   __t__

B.   Check the words to make sure they appear in the correct alphabetical order.

Review

Skill: Proofread for grammar, usage, punctuation, and capitalization

Materials: Transparency of "Independence Day Celebrations" (page 54)
Overhead pen

Lesson:

1. Explain that the students will review some of the skills they have practiced in previous lessons.

2. Show part A of "Independence Day Celebrations" on the overhead projector and read it aloud. Ask:

   Q *What do you notice in this passage?*

   Point out that the passage includes many errors.

3. Model finding and correcting the first few errors; then ask:

   Q *Where else do you see an error? What should we do to fix that error?*

   As the students respond, make corrections on the transparency, using the editing marks you have established with your class. (See "Independence Day Celebrations: Corrections" on the facing page.)

4. Read part B aloud. Use the students' suggestions to write a passage about a holiday. Stop to have the students explain why certain punctuation, capitalization, or word forms are needed.

5. (Optional) Have the students write their own passages. Then have them work in pairs to read each other's passages, search for errors, and correct them.

6. (Optional) Ask the students to open to *Student Skill Practice Book* page 65. Read the directions aloud and have the students work individually or in pairs on the activity. For additional practice with this skill, assign the activities on pages 66–68 of the *Student Skill Practice Book*. (For corrections for these activities, see pages 88–89 of the *Skill Practice Teaching Guide*.)

Independence Day Celebrations: Corrections

A. **Corrections are given below. Corrections for the final sentence may vary.**

       isn't   I   D
Ours ~~isnt~~ the only country to celebrate ~~independence~~ ~~day~~.

                  have
Many countries ~~has~~ a special day on which to honor their nation.

C   *celebrate* C   D   J
~~canadians~~ ~~celebrates~~ ~~canada~~ ~~day~~ every ~~july~~ 1. They get the day off

               have   A   *celebrate* A   D
from work and ~~has~~ picnics. ~~australians~~ ~~celebrates~~ ~~australia~~ ~~day~~ on

J   M   I   D   S
~~january~~ 26. ~~mexican~~ ~~independence~~ ~~day~~ is ~~september~~ 16. Many

              have   *parties*
Mexican people ~~has~~ big fiestas, or ~~partys~~, where they dance⊙eat⊙

                    I   D *day for people to come together*
and talk. Around the world, ~~independence~~ ~~day~~ is an important.

B. **Check for the appropriate use of the practiced skills in the passage.**

Blackline Masters

An Acrobatic Ape

A.   Underline the nouns in the passage below, as shown.

A <u>gibbon</u> is a small ape from Asia. It lives in the forest. It has long arms and no tail. It can grasp and carry things with its hands and feet.

Gibbons live in families, with a mother, a father, and offspring (children). They eat mostly fruit. They eat other things, too, including flowers, leaves, insects, spiders, and birds. They do not build nests like other apes. Instead, they sleep sitting up between branches. They use their arms to swing from tree to tree. They can also leap between trees. They are so quick and graceful that almost no predator can catch them.

B.   Write a short passage using interesting nouns. Underline the nouns.

The Haunted House

A. **Underline the adjectives in the passage below, as shown. Add a few adjectives to the passage.**

No one has lived in the <u>haunted</u> house for many years. It sits behind an old, white fence with a broken gate at the top of a hill. Only brave children dare to tiptoe through the weed-filled yard, up the cracked steps, and onto the sagging porch. Braver children peer through the windows. The bravest children open the door and step into the dark hall. When they do, they're sure to hear a sound that chills their bones, the sound of a voice singing a song.

B. **Write a short passage using interesting adjectives. Underline the adjectives.**

How to Make S'mores

A.   Underline the verbs in the passage below, as shown.

<u>To prepare</u> s'mores, you will need a campfire, a stick, marshmallows, graham crackers, and a chocolate bar. Poke the stick through a marshmallow. With an adult nearby, hold the stick over the campfire. Toast the marshmallow until it is golden brown. Remove the marshmallow from the stick and smash it down on a graham cracker. Place a piece of chocolate on top of the marshmallow. Put another graham cracker on top. Enjoy your s'more—and then make some more!

B.   Write a short "how to" passage using interesting verbs. Underline the verbs.

Mountains of Sand

A.   **Combine the following words to make contractions.**

are not   he will   I am   they are

B.   **Write out the words that make the following contractions.**

shouldn't   I'll   it's   she's

C.   **Underline the contractions in the paragraph below. Write the words that make each contraction above it, as shown.**

I am
I'm getting ready to go on a trip. My mom said to pack light

because she isn't going to carry my bag for me. I don't want

to forget anything. We're going to visit some sand dunes in

Colorado. From what I've heard, they're giant mountains of sand.

My dad said he's going to ski down the dunes. I hope he doesn't

hurt himself. I can't ski, but I think he'll let me sled down instead.

I didn't know that it's possible to ski and sled on sand.

How the Platypus Got Its Nose

A. Underline incomplete sentences in the passage below. Use a caret to add text to make the sentences complete, as shown.

One day a platypus was walking along the riverbed, minding

his own business. <u>His long, round nose</u>ˆ hopped right on his nose.
sniffed at the ground

The startled platypus. Perhaps that is how the platypus got a nose

like a duck's bill.

B. Write a short passage starting with the sentence below. Write complete sentences.

One day a kangaroo came hopping along.

A Visit to the Museum

A. Write the names of the nouns you see in the picture. Write both the singular and plural forms of the noun, as shown.

Singular	*Plural*
1. student	students
2.	
3.	
4.	
5.	
6.	
7.	

B. Write a short passage using at least four of the plural nouns listed above. The passage can be about the picture or another topic. Underline the plural nouns in the passage.

What I Want to Be

A. Underline the verbs in the passage below and mark whether they are in past (*pa*), present (*pr*), or future (*f*) tense, as shown.

When I <u>was</u> little, I said, "I will be a veterinarian someday." I read books about vets. I asked my dog's vet questions about her work.

Now I tell everyone, "I will be a writer." I read the "About the Author" sections in books. I carry a notepad and jot down my ideas as they pop into my head. I write stories and poems and show them to my family.

Later on, though, maybe I will decide that I will be something else entirely. Maybe I will consider a career as a firefighter or forest ranger. Maybe I will have more than one career. That way I will fulfill at least a few of my dreams.

B. Write three short paragraphs like those above, using past, present, and future verb tenses.

My Sister the Space Alien

A. **Underline each incorrect verb in the passage below and write the correct verb above it, as shown.**

Sometimes my sister <u>pretend</u> *pretends* to be from outer space. She move her arms and legs stiffly, like a robot. She invent strange words like "oogle-boogle." My brother and I laughs. When my parents says, "Time for bed," my sister just say, "Munka-munka-munka." When they tells her, "Clean your room," she respond, "Frzzz-frzzz-frzzz." They stands there and scratches their heads. They does not understand space alien language.

B. **Write a sentence for each of the verbs, as shown.**

play   *I play softball with my family.*

plays   *He plays the trumpet in the school band.*

is   _____

are   _____

move _____

moves _____

We Love Our Pets

A. **Complete each set of sentences with pronouns that match the word in bold, as shown.**

1. **Jaya** loves Max, ____her____ pet mouse. Max loves ____her____.

    ____She____ is glad that Max is ____hers____.

2. **Benjy** loves Max, _____ pet mouse. Max loves _____.

    _____ is glad that Max is _____.

3. **Lee and Lisa** love Max, _____ pet mouse. Max loves

    _____. _____ are glad that Max is _____.

4. **My family** loves Max, _____ pet mouse. Max loves

    _____. _____ are glad that Max is _____.

B. **Rewrite each sentence below by replacing the words in bold with the correct pronoun. Then add a new sentence with a pronoun in it, as shown.**

1. **Max** likes to eat **mushrooms**.

    He likes to eat them. They taste good.

2. **Max and I** play with **marbles**.

    _____

Fast and Heavy

A. **Look at the information in the chart. Then complete each sentence using words that end with *er* or *est*.**

Animal	Maximum Speed	Maximum Weight
Cheetah	70 MPH	140 pounds
Coyote	43 MPH	50 pounds
Giraffe	32 MPH	4250 pounds

1. The giraffe is **fast**.

   The coyote is ___*faster*___ than the giraffe.

   The cheetah is the _____ of them all.

2. The coyote is **heavy**.

   The cheetah is _____ than the coyote.

   The giraffe is the _____ of them all.

B. **Add *er* or *est* to two of the words below. Write a short paragraph using the new words.**

quick   short   slow   speedy

The Letters of Sun and Moon

A. Circle the commas in the date, greeting, and closing of the letter below.

January 31, 2010

Dear Moon,

I miss you. I try to stay up until you arrive each evening. Most of the time, though, you don't show up till past my bedtime.

Sincerely,

Sun

B. Add commas where needed in the letter below.

February 17 2010

Dear Sun

I miss you, too. It does get chilly up here without you. But I do love the peace, quiet, and darkness of nighttime, when almost everyone's asleep.

Your friend

Moon

C. Write more letters between Sun and Moon. Use commas as needed.

A Cooperative Cactus

A.   Read the passage below and notice how the commas are used in a series.

Some see the desert as a empty, lonely, and lifeless place. Yet the desert is full of plants and animals working together to stay alive. The saguaro cactus is a good example. It provides food, shade, and shelter for many creatures.

B.   Add the missing commas in the passage below.

Coyotes foxes squirrels and other animals eat its red fruit and tiny, black seeds. They sit in its shade to cool off. Gila woodpeckers peck holes in its sides to live in. These "hotel rooms" are used by other animals such as insects bats and rats when the woodpeckers move out. Humans use the long, straight rods inside the saguaro to make roofs fences and fuel.

C.   Write two or three sentences using commas in a series.

The Bad Joke

A. **Put quotation marks before and after spoken words, as shown in the first sentence.**

"Nico, do you want to hear a joke?"asked Kim.

Sure, said Nico.

What should you do to a blue elephant? asked Kim.

I don't know, Nico replied. What should you do to a blue

elephant?

Kim answered, You should try to cheer him up!

That is a really bad joke, said Nico.

It is not bad. It is funny! exclaimed Kim.

If you want to hear a funny joke, I'll tell you one, said Nico.

B. **Continue writing a few more sentences of the dialogue between Kim and Nico. Use quotation marks to show speech.**

Randy's Burgers

A. Underline words that use apostrophes to show that something belongs to someone or something else, as shown.

<u>Randy's</u> Restaurant is famous for its hamburgers. The waiters' trays are even shaped like burgers. The restaurant's specialty is the Randy Burger. It is a giant hamburger with lettuce, tomato, cheese, and pickles. Randy picks the vegetables from his neighbor's garden. He uses his family's secret recipe to make the hamburger patties.

B. Write sentences that contain 's or ' using one word from each column below, as shown.

Randy	hamburger	delicious
Rhonda	shakes	thick
The customers	stomachs	full

1. <u>*Rhonda's hamburger is delicious.*</u>

2. _____

3. _____

The Boston Marathon

A.   Underline the proper nouns in the passage below.

The <u>Boston Marathon</u> is held every Patriot's Day in Boston, Massachusetts. The first Boston Marathon was run on Monday, April 19, 1897. There were 15 runners at the start, and 10 finished. Now, thousands of runners come from all over the world to compete in the race. In 2007 one runner competed from space! Astronaut Sunita Williams ran the marathon while in orbit on the International Space Station. She circled the Earth at least twice while running the 26.2 miles on a treadmill.

B.   For each proper noun underlined above, write the type of proper noun it is, as shown below.

- special events
- days of the week

C.   Choose two different types of proper nouns from the list above. Write five examples for each type, as shown.

- days of the week: Monday, Tuesday, Wednesday, Thursday, Friday

A Place for Everything

A. Put the following words in alphabetical order. The letters in the boxes will answer the riddle below!

queen   **1.**

quart   **2.**

sting   **3.**

quiet   **4.**

silly   **5.** _____ _____ ☐ _____

sight   **6.** _____ ☐ _____ _____ _____

What do you call a porcupine wrapped in a blanket?

____ ____ ____ ____ ____ ____

B. Write any three words that would appear in a dictionary between the words below. Write them in alphabetical order.

1. black _____ *blue, brown, gray* _____ green

2. pancakes _____ waffles

3. bee _____ grasshopper

Independence Day Celebrations

A.   Read the passage. Identify and correct the errors.

Ours isnt the only country to celebrate independence day. Many countries has a special day on which to honor their nation. canadians celebrates canada day every july 1. They get the day off from work and has picnics. australians celebrates australia day on january 26. mexican independence day is september 16. Many Mexican people has big fiestas, or partys, where they dance eat and talk. Around the world, independence day is an important.

B.   Write a passage about a holiday. Proofread it for correctness.

Student Skill Practice Book Corrections

Presidents and Pets: Corrections

A. **Nouns are underlined in the passage below.**

Many presidents had pets. Woodrow Wilson

had sheep. Calvin Coolidge had a raccoon. He used

a leash and took it for a walk every day. Theodore

Roosevelt had guinea pigs, snakes, and a badger.

Once, Roosevelt's son took his pony in the elevator.

Another time, he put snakes on his father's desk!

Today, you can see two Scottish terrier dogs

playing at the White House.

B. **Check for the appropriate use of nouns in the passage.**

The Perfect Pie: Corrections

A. **Nouns are underlined in the passage below.**

Jason loved to bake. He started with cookies and

muffins. Then he made a pie. Once Jason started

to make pies, he could not stop. He filled them

with jelly, chocolate bars, and ice cream. He put

everything into pies!

Once, Jason baked a pie with the worst foods he

could think of. It had peas, custard, scrambled eggs,

and fish. It looked perfect. He decided to save it for

his sister's birthday lunch.

B. **Check for the appropriate use of nouns in the passage.**

A Winter Survivor: Corrections

A. Nouns are underlined in the passage below.

The emperor penguin lives in Antarctica. It has a

white belly and a black coat.

In winter, Antarctica is very cold. There are

storms and howling winds. Penguins stand close

together to stay warm. They take turns standing on

the outside of the group where it is coldest. They

must share their warmth to live.

B. Check for the appropriate use of nouns in the passage.

The Gentle Giant: Corrections

A. Nouns are underlined in the passage below.

Mrs. Mosley has a dog called Dudley. Dudley is

the size of a horse. He could swallow your arm. He

could probably swallow your bike. Mrs. Mosley calls

him the Gentle Giant.

Dudley is different from other dogs. He wears

clothes! Last week, he was wearing a blue poncho.

Yesterday, he was in a purple sweater and a hat. I feel

sorry for him. He is huge and he has terrible taste in

clothes.

B. Check for the appropriate use of nouns in the passage.

The Smallest Turtle: Corrections

A. Adjectives are underlined, and examples of additional adjectives are given.

The Speckled Turtle of South Africa is the

natural

smallest turtle in the ˄ world. It hides under rocky

, dark

shelves and in tight ˄ places. It has a flat, orange-

spotted

brown shell with tiny spots. The ˄ shell is the same

little

color as the ground, so the ˄ turtle is difficult for

tiny

sharp-eyed birds to see. The ˄ turtle hides when it

sees a hungry bird, or it lifts itself up on its tall legs

and runs.

B. Check for the appropriate use of adjectives in the passage.

Piping Up: Corrections

A. Adjectives are underlined, and examples of additional adjectives are given.

Scottish

The ˄ bagpipe is a strange instrument. It has a

metal

soft, leather bag and lots of ˄ pipes. When a player

blows into a pipe and presses the bag, you hear two

different sounds. One is a low, steady, groaning

big

sound. It is like a ˄ swarm of angry bees. The other

sound is the shrill, shrieking song. The bagpipe is a

difficult instrument to learn. But a bagpipe makes a

beautiful sound.

B. Check for the appropriate use of adjectives in the passage.

The Pie Contest: Corrections

A. Adjectives are underlined, and examples of additional adjectives are given.

      blueberry
Jason made a <u>perfect</u> ˄pie for the <u>baking</u> contest.

He wanted to win a <u>blue</u> ribbon for his <u>golden</u>,

<u>crispy, perfect</u> pie.

          long
Jason walked into the ˄hall with his pie. He saw a
lumpy,
˄<u>round</u> object flying through the air. He ducked. He

ducked again. Pies were flying everywhere! Jason

groaned loudly. This was a <u>pie-throwing</u> contest,

not a <u>pie-baking</u> contest. He would have to take his
        warm
<u>wonderful</u>, ˄pie somewhere else—and quickly.

B. Check for the appropriate use of adjectives in the passage.

New Trousers: Corrections

A. Adjectives are underlined, and examples of additional adjectives are given.

Anna's dad needed <u>new</u> trousers. The <u>old</u> ones fit,
    big   *front*
but there were ˄holes in the ˄pockets that swallowed

his <u>heavy</u> keys.
     color
Anna drew a ˄picture of some <u>amazing</u> trousers.

They would have <u>four</u>, <u>deep</u> pockets. That was <u>one</u>
     new
pocket for each of her dad's keys. The ˄trousers

would also be <u>waterproof</u> and <u>heatproof</u>. Then, her
poor
˄dad wouldn't get burned when he spilled <u>hot</u> coffee.

They might not be the <u>latest</u> fashion, but they

would be much more <u>practical</u> than the <u>old</u> pair.

B. Check for the appropriate use of adjectives in the passage.

The Show: Corrections

A. Verbs are underlined in the passage below.

I crouch on the edge of the swimming pool. Goose bumps prickle my skin. My sisters watch and giggle.

First, I jump up and down one hundred times. Then I kick my legs. Finally, I dance. My sisters clap their hands. Finally, I am ready. I look at my sisters. I don't believe it. My sisters ran away! After all that, they didn't stay for the dive.

B. Check for the appropriate use of verbs in the passage.

You Are Feeling Sleepy: Corrections

A. Verbs are underlined in the passage below.

What happens when you sleep? Your muscles relax. Your heart slows. When you fall into a deep sleep, your eyelids flicker as if you are watching a movie. You are dreaming! As you dream, your brain imagines that you are meeting a movie star, giving a speech, or fighting monsters at school. Some people say that dreams help the brain to learn, understand, and remember.

B. Check for the appropriate use of verbs in the passage.

The Great Escape: Corrections

A.   Verbs are underlined in the passage below.

Pablo leaped onto his skateboard and zoomed down the path. He looked back. There were three monsters following him! They were moving fast. Pablo's heart pounded as he skated into a clearing. Suddenly, he skidded to a stop. A cliff!

Pablo had no choice. He knew he couldn't fight all the monsters with his bare hands. He gulped, squeezed his eyes shut, and skated over the cliff. The wind whistled in his ears. Finally, he thudded to the earth. As he sped away, he looked back. The monsters watched from the cliff top. Their eyes bulged with rage. Pablo laughed. He had made it!

B.   Check for the appropriate use of verbs in the passage.

The Best Medicine: Corrections

A.   Verbs are underlined in the passage below.

We all laugh. Some people cackle. Some giggle. Some chuckle. And some roar. Laughter is good for you. When you laugh, your face relaxes, and a feeling of happiness flows through your body. Laughter is good exercise, but you don't need to get up from your chair!

To stay healthy, include some laughter in your day. Here are some ideas: 1) Read a comic. 2) Watch a funny movie. 3) Make funny faces at yourself in the mirror.

B.   Check for the appropriate use of verbs in the passage.

Zac's Bad Day: Corrections

A. Answers are shown below.

are not	we are	he will	she is
aren't	we're	he'll	she's

B. Answers are shown below.

can't	they're	I'll	he's
cannot	they are	I will	he is

C. Contractions are underlined. The words that make each contraction are written above it.

Zac was having a bad day. He *could not* couldn't find
anything to do. He blew bubbles. He checked to see
if there was any food floating around. There *was not* wasn't.
He had He'd thought that his friend Big was coming to visit.
But Zac *had not* hadn't seen Big all morning. Big *would not* wouldn't
lie, would he?

Zac drifted to the bottom of his tank. He stared
sadly through the glass into Big's bedroom. If only
there were some other goldfish around here!

13

Speaking Up: Corrections

A. Answers are shown below.

do not	I am	they will	it is
don't	I'm	they'll	it's

B. Answers are shown below.

won't	we're	she'll	he'd
will not	we are	she will	he would

C. Contractions are underlined. The words that make each contraction are written above it.

Celia has to give a speech. *She is* She's worried, even
though *it is* it's two weeks away. She knows exactly what
will happen. People will shout that they *cannot* can't hear her.
They will They'll wriggle in their seats. *That is* That's what happened
the last time Celia gave a speech. But Celia's voice
will not won't go any louder. *She will* She'll try to speak up this time,
but there *is not* isn't a volume knob on her voice.

14 | Being a Writer™

One Day at a Time: Corrections

A. Answers are shown below.

I would	do not	they have	does not
I'd	*don't*	*they've*	*doesn't*

B. Answers are shown below.

didn't	wouldn't	it'll	we've
did not	*would not*	*it will*	*we have*

C. Contractions are underlined. The words that make each contraction are written above it.

An Italian man named Antonio Todde lived to be
was not
112 years old. It wasn't easy living that long. Antonio
did not
had to look after himself. He didn't stay up late.
he would
He didn't eat junk food. Every day, he'd go for a ride
did not
on his bicycle. Antonio also had a peaceful life. He
was not
wasn't hit by falling roof tiles or chased by bears.
he would
Just before he died, he said he'd like to live for a

few more years.

Mona Lisa: Corrections

A. Answers are shown below.

they have	she has	you will	I am
they've	*she's*	*you'll*	*I'm*

B. Answers are shown below.

shouldn't	they've	isn't	they'd
should not	*they have*	*is not*	*they would*

C. Contractions are underlined. The words that make each contraction are written above it.

You have
The Mona Lisa is a famous painting. You've
There is
probably seen it. There's a woman in the painting.
you are
Wherever you're standing, her eyes follow you. The
painting is in a museum in Paris, France. It hangs
cannot   *It is*
inside a glass box so that people can't touch it. It's
hard to know why people like Mona Lisa so much.
it is
Maybe it's her smile.

Heads Up: Corrections

A. Incomplete sentences are underlined. Inserted text will vary. Examples are shown below.

A helmet *protects*
~~Protects~~ a person's head. That's why you wear
one when you are climbing up a mountain, playing
ice hockey, or riding a *bike*. In the Middle Ages, knights *wore helmets*.
The helmet covered the knight's whole head. There
were only tiny eye holes for the knight to *see through*. Inside
the helmet, it *was very hot*. But it was much better for a knight to
have a red face than to *lose his head*.

B. Check for the use of complete sentences in the passage.

Great Plans: Corrections

A. Incomplete sentences are underlined. Inserted text will vary. Examples are shown below.

It was the last day of the holidays. There was
nothing to do. *Stewart and I felt* ~~Felt~~ bored. Stewart said we should
build a fort. We would use the dining room table.
To make a roof, *we* pulled sheets and blankets over the
table. When the fort was finished, we *crawled in*. Inside the
fort, it was dark and quiet. We sat there for a few
minutes. "This is boring," we said at the same time.

B. Check for the use of complete sentences in the passage.

Cats and Dogs: Corrections

A. Incomplete sentences are underlined. Inserted text will vary. Examples are shown below.

Ramon had a problem. Cats followed him

everywhere. Every time he walked home from school,
Followed him   *But he already*
cats, Ramon liked cats. Already had a cat named
He told
Josephine at home. Told the new cats to go away, but
still Followed him   *was not happy*
the cats. When Josephine saw the new cats, she.

B. Check for the use of complete sentences in the passage.

Towns and Cities: Corrections

A. Incomplete sentences are underlined. Inserted text will vary. Examples are shown below.

A ghost town is a town where nobody lives.

Once, the streets were full of people. But today no
are empty
lives there   are quiet
one. The streets. Houses and buildings.

Some ghost towns are near abandoned gold
once dug For gold
mines, where people. Others are in oil fields where
once drilled For oil
people. But when the mines were empty and the oil
left
fields ran dry, the people.

B. Check for the use of complete sentences in the passage.

The Classroom: Corrections

A. Answers may vary.

Singular	Plural
1. pencil	pencils
2. coat	coats
3. chair	chairs
4. shelf	shelves
5. book	books
6. plant	plants
7. desk	desks

B. Check for the appropriate use of plural nouns in the passage.

Dad's Study Room: Corrections

A. Answers may vary.

Singular	Plural
1. rug	rugs
2. photo	photos
3. box	boxes
4. computer	computers
5. umbrella	umbrellas
6. chair	chairs
7. bookshelf	bookshelves

B. Check for the appropriate use of plural nouns in the passage.

In the Forest: Corrections

A. **Answers may vary.**

	Singular	Plural
1.	weed	weeds
2.	deer	deer
3.	mouse	mice
4.	leaf	leaves
5.	wolf	wolves
6.	bush	bushes
7.	mosquito	mosquitoes

B. **Check for the appropriate use of plural nouns in the passage.**

Camping Out: Corrections

A. **Answers may vary.**

	Singular	Plural
1.	marshmallow	marshmallows
2.	tent	tents
3.	log	logs
4.	Flame	Flames
5.	raccoon	raccoons
6.	match	matches
7.	scarf	scarves

B. **Check for the appropriate use of plural nouns in the passage.**

The Kitchen: Corrections

A. Verbs are underlined and marked to signify past (pa), present (pr), or future (f) tense.

Last week, the kitchen floor *pa*disappeared. When I *pa*looked down, I *pa*saw the dirt under our house. When I *pa*crawled down, I *pa*found a toy car I *pa*lost months ago.

Today, there *pr*is a new kitchen floor. But now there *pr*is no ceiling! I *pr*watch the sky as I *pr*chew on a sandwich. Dark clouds *pr*are bunching together. It *pr*is funny how you *pr*don't think about the sky unless you *pr*have no ceiling.

Maybe it *f*will rain tomorrow. My toast *f*will get soggy, but I *f*won't mind too much. It *f*will be the only time I *f*will eat breakfast indoors and in the rain at the same time.

B. Check for the appropriate use of past, present, and future verb tenses in the three paragraphs.

Blue Jeans: Corrections

A. Verbs are underlined and marked to signify past (pa), present (pr), or future (f) tense.

Italians *pa*made the first pair of jeans. They *pa*made jeans for sailors. When the sailors *pa*crouched down and *pa*scrubbed the decks of the ship, they *pa*rolled up the legs of their jeans. They *pa*washed their jeans in nets that they *pa*dragged behind the ship.

Today, there *pr*are jeans of many sizes and styles. All kinds of people *pr*wear jeans because they *pr*are so comfortable.

In the future, maybe you *f*will travel to different countries. Maybe you *f*will sail out to sea. You *f*will look fine in a pair of jeans no matter what.

B. Check for the appropriate use of past, present, and future verb tenses in the three paragraphs.

A White World: Corrections

A. **Verbs are underlined and marked to signify past (*pa*), present (*pr*), or future (*f*) tense.**

Two hundred years ago, Antarctica was an unknown land. When people first explored it, they saw penguins, seals, and whales. They faced cold winds and lived through long, black nights.

Today, ships plow through the ice and bring people and supplies. Scientists work all year long. Tourists visit in the summer.

One day, scientists will learn more about Antarctica. Then we will understand how to protect this beautiful, white world.

B. **Check for the appropriate use of past, present, and future verb tenses in the three paragraphs.**

The Banjo Player: Corrections

A. **Verbs are underlined and marked to signify past (*pa*), present (*pr*), or future (*f*) tense.**

On the street below my house, a boy played the banjo. Then he sang a song. His voice trembled. The boy sounded tired.

He is playing this morning. I put on a coat and go downstairs. I throw a coin into his hat. The boy grins. He scoops up the hat and puts it on. Then he lifts the banjo over his shoulder and walks away.

The street will be dull without music. Perhaps the boy will play somewhere else. Tomorrow, I will go for a walk. I will look for him.

B. **Check for the appropriate use of past, present, and future verb tenses in the three paragraphs.**

The Running of the Bulls: Corrections

A. Incorrect verbs are underlined, and the correct verbs are written above.

Every year in Spain, the people of Pamplona
wake
wakes to the sound of a horn. When they hears it,
hear
know
they knows that the most famous and dangerous day

of the year has begun. It is the Running of the Bulls!

Bulls run down the streets of Pamplona. People
dash
dashes in front of them, running as fast as they can.
stops
Sometimes a bull stop running and charge the people
charges
have
watching. People has been killed. But that do not
does

stop people from watching every year.

B. Check for subject-verb agreement in the sentences.

The Movie Buff: Corrections

A. Incorrect verbs are underlined, and the correct verbs are written above.

has
Sally has a job in a movie theater. She have to

spend a lot of time standing in the dark, watching

the same movies over and over again.

watches
When she watch movies for the first time,
holds
she hold her breath as she watch exciting car chases
watches
and action. She lean forward in her chair when
leans
sees
she see robots, dinosaurs, and special effects. But

after watching the same movie for the fifth time,

she gets bored!

B. Check for subject-verb agreement in the sentences.

Marathon of the Sands: Corrections

A. **Incorrect verbs are underlined, and the correct verbs are written above.**

Every year, people goes _[go]_ to the Sahara Desert to run a race. It's called the Marathon of the Sands. Does _[Do]_ you feel like a challenge? This is what you face. You runs _[run]_ 143 miles over hot sand. You carries _[carry]_ your gear, including a flashlight for running at night. At first, your pack do not _[does not]_ feel heavy. But as the miles rolls _[roll]_ on, the straps hurt your shoulders. Your back aches. The sun blaze _[blazes]_ down on your head. Sometimes, you run with a crowd. Other times, you is _[are]_ alone. You does not _[do not]_ see another runner anywhere.

B. **Check for subject-verb agreement in the sentences.**

Missing: Corrections

A. **Incorrect verbs are underlined, and the correct verbs are written above.**

LOST: One large white cat named Menace.

Our cat Menace is missing. He are _[is]_ white all over except for an orange patch over one eye. His eyes is _[are]_ yellow. Part of his tail is missing. Menace like _[likes]_ to go _[goes]_ exploring and can't find his way home again. Sometimes somebody fall in _[falls]_ love with him and decides to take him home. We is _[are]_ missing him very much.

B. **Check for subject-verb agreement in the sentences.**

Shirley: Corrections

A.   The correct pronouns are shown below.

1. **Fred** knows this elephant, Shirley. When Shirley is bored, she knocks on ___his___ bedroom window and takes ___him___ for a ride.

2. **I** know this elephant, Shirley. When Shirley is bored, she knocks on ___my___ bedroom window and takes ___me___ for a ride.

3. **Jacob and I** know this elephant, Shirley. When Shirley is bored, she knocks on ___our___ bedroom window and takes ___us___ for a ride.

B.   Revised sentences are shown below. The second sentences will vary.

1. **Shirley** ran away from **the circus.**
She ran away from it. She was not happy there.

2. **Shirley** likes to eat **chocolate bars.**
She likes to eat them. They taste good.

Writing the Story: Corrections

A.   The correct pronouns are shown below.

1. **I** am writing a story about ___my___ amazing adventure. ___I___ am making it up as ___I___ go. No one's story is as amazing as ___mine___.

2. **The Smith brothers** are writing a story about ___their___ amazing adventure. ___They___ are making it up as ___they___ go. No one's story is as amazing as ___theirs___.

B.   Revised sentences are shown below. The second sentences will vary.

1. **The story** was ten pages long.
It was ten pages long. It was an amazing personal narrative.

2. **My classmates** liked **the story.**
They liked it. They thought it was interesting.

3. **My dad** fell asleep when I read **the story.**
He fell asleep when I read it. He was tired.

Being in a Movie: Corrections

A. The correct pronouns are shown below.

1. **You** love movies. _Your_ favorite movies have dramatic music. When _you_ run fast, _you_ imagine _yourself_ being in a movie with music playing around _you_ .

2. **Manuel** loves movies. _His_ favorite movies have dramatic music. When _he_ runs fast, _he_ imagines _himself_ being in a movie with music playing around _him_ .

B. Revised sentences are shown below. The second sentences will vary.

1. **You and I** should see the movie.
   We should see it. It will be great.

2. **My parents** say the movie will be silly.
   They say it will be silly. They are wrong!

Learning Guitar: Corrections

A. The correct pronouns are shown below.

1. **Darnell** is teaching _himself_ to play the guitar. _His_ friend Matt tried to teach _him_ , but Matt's taste in music is different from _his_ .

2. **You** are teaching _yourself_ to play the guitar. _Your_ friend Matt tried to teach _you_ , but Matt's taste in music is different from _yours_ .

3. **Jenny and I** are teaching _ourselves_ to play the guitar. _Our_ friend Matt tried to teach _us_ , but Matt's taste in music is different from _ours_ .

B. Revised sentences are shown below. The second sentences will vary.

1. **The guitar** has a broken string.
   It has a broken string. I will play it anyway.

2. **My sister and I** take turns playing the guitar.
   We take turns playing it. We both like playing.

Smelly, Clean, and Clear: Corrections

A. Corrections are given below.

smelly

1. Hugh's feet are ___smelly___ .

Hugh's feet are ___smellier___ than his socks.

Hugh's feet are the ___smelliest___ of all.

clean

2. The shirt is ___clean___ .

The shirt is ___cleaner___ than the socks.

The shirt is the ___cleanest___ of all.

clear

3. The water is ___clear___ .

The water is ___clearer___ than the mud.

The water is the ___clearest___ of all.

B. Check for the appropriate use of comparative and superlative adjectives in the passage.

Loud, Quiet, and Shiny: Corrections

A. Corrections are given below.

loud

1. The stereo is ___loud___ .

The stereo is ___louder___ than the piano.

The stereo is the ___loudest___ of all.

quiet

2. The mouse is ___quiet___ .

The mouse is ___quieter___ than the cat.

The mouse is the ___quietest___ of all.

shiny

3. The car is ___shiny___ .

The car is ___shinier___ than the truck.

The car is the ___shiniest___ of all.

B. Check for the appropriate use of comparative and superlative adjectives in the passage.

Lonely, Empty, and Full: Corrections

A. Corrections are given below.

lonely

1. The desert is ___lonely___.

   The desert is ___lonelier___ than the mountain.

   The desert is the ___loneliest___ of all.

empty

2. The haunted house is ___empty___.

   The haunted house is ___emptier___ than my house.

   The haunted house is the ___emptiest___ of all.

full

3. The jug is ___full___.

   The jug is ___fuller___ than the cup.

   The jug is the ___fullest___ of all.

B. Check for the appropriate use of comparative and superlative adjectives in the passage.

Happy, Busy, and Soft: Corrections

A. Corrections are given below.

happy

1. Davia is ___happy___.

   Davia is ___happier___ than her sister.

   Davia is the ___happiest___ of all.

busy

2. The city is ___busy___.

   The city is ___busier___ than the village.

   The city is the ___busiest___ of all.

soft

3. The pillow is ___soft___.

   The pillow is ___softer___ than the bed.

   The pillow is the ___softest___ of all.

B. Check for the appropriate use of comparative and superlative adjectives in the passage.

The Letters of Dog and Flea: Corrections

A.   Commas are circled in the date, greeting, and closing.

August 9, 2010

Dear Flea,

Sometimes I enjoy your company. However,
I think it is time for you to leave.

Sincerely,

Itchy Dog

B.   Correct use of commas is shown below.

August 10, 2010

Dear Dog,

I enjoy your company, too. My friends and I all
like it here, so we're staying.

Your friend,

Flea

C.   Check for the appropriate use of commas in the date, greeting, and closing of the written letter.

The Letters of Grant and Sally: Corrections

A.   Commas are circled in the date, greeting, and closing.

March 18, 2010

Dear Sally,

Last night, I made 15 chocolate mini-muffins.
This morning, they were gone!

Your brother,

Grant

B.   Correct use of commas is shown below.

March 18, 2010

Dear Grant,

I saw Dad tiptoeing out of the kitchen. He had
crumbs on his face.

Your sister,

Sally

C.   Check for the appropriate use of commas in the date, greeting, and closing of the written letter.

The Letters of Grisham and Felix: Corrections

A. Commas are circled in the date, greeting, and closing.

May 2, 2010

Dear Felix,

Jemma wants to join our club. I told her that it's No Girls Allowed, but she said it's not a real club unless girls can join, too.

Your friend,

Grisham

B. Correct use of commas is shown below.

May 2, 2010

Dear Grisham,

Jemma can join the club, but we should change the rules to Only Cool Girls Allowed!

Your friend,

Felix

C. Check for the appropriate use of commas in the date, greeting, and closing of the written letter.

The Letters of Sonia and Shoes: Corrections

A. Commas are circled in the date, greeting, and closing.

July 2, 2010

Dear Shoes,

Next week, I will run a very hard race. I hope I can count on you to make a big effort!

Sincerely,

Sonia

B. Correct use of commas is shown below.

July 2, 2010

Dear Sonia,

I have been working too hard for the last six months. My soles are worn down and my laces keep coming undone.

Yours truly,

Shoes

C. Check for the appropriate use of commas in the date, greeting, and closing of the written letter.

The Designer: Corrections

B. **Correct use of commas is shown below.**

My mom's work room is full of pirate hats, silly glasses, and rock star wigs. Dresses, jackets, and coats lie on the floor in brightly colored heaps. Mom's latest costume is a giant bird. It has purple feathers, an orange beak, and eyes made from glass. My friends say my mom has a weird job, but I think she's amazing.

C. **Check for the appropriate use of commas in a series in the sentences.**

The Pancake Show: Corrections

B. **Correct use of commas is shown below.**

Each time I put on a pancake show, Samantha gets maple syrup from the pantry. Trudy cuts a banana, and Edwin puts plates on the table. Then my friends watch and wait. They stare at the pancakes. They lick their lips, and rub their hands together. Maybe they're not interested in the show at all. Maybe they are more interested in eating the performers.

C. **Check for the appropriate use of commas in a series in the sentences.**

Nat King Cole: Corrections

B. **Correct use of commas is shown below.**

Nat King Cole loved jazz music. So he started a jazz band. One friend played guitar○another friend played bass guitar○and Nat played piano and sang. Nat felt shy about singing, but many people said he had a great voice.

C. **Check for the appropriate use of commas in a series in the sentences.**

Origami: Corrections

B. **Correct use of commas is shown below.**

People do origami all over the world. They make butterflies○elephants○and lilies. One of the most popular shapes to make is the crane. A crane is a bird with a long○thin○and curvy neck.

C. **Check for the appropriate use of commas in a series in the sentences.**

Toni and Mrs. Crowe: Corrections

A. Correct use of quotation marks is shown below.

"Why is New York called the Big Apple?" asked Toni.

"I don't know," said Mrs. Crowe.

"Maybe everyone in New York really likes apples," said Toni.

"Maybe it rains apple juice in New York," said Mrs. Crowe.

"Maybe all the houses are made from apples," said Toni.

"Maybe we should go to New York and see for ourselves," said Toni.

B. Check for the appropriate use of quotation marks in the dialogue.

Jack and the Daisy: Corrections

A. Correct use of quotation marks is shown below.

"Please don't pick me, Jack," said the daisy.

"I didn't know daisies could talk," said Jack.

"Well, this daisy can, so please don't pick me," said the daisy.

"I'm sorry, but I have to pick you. My sister isn't well and I thought a daisy might cheer her up," said Jack.

"I have an idea," said the daisy.

"What is it?" asked Jack.

"Plant me in a flowerpot and I'll live in your sister's room forever," said the daisy.

B. Check for the appropriate use of quotation marks in the dialogue.

Bella and Her Dad: Corrections

A. Proper use of quotation marks is shown below.

"Dad, can I go to a rock concert on Friday night?"

asked Bella.

"No," said her dad.

"Please, Dad! It will be amazing."

"What makes you so sure?" asked her dad.

"There's a man who plays a guitar with one

hundred strings," said Bella.

"Really? That *does* sound amazing," said her dad.

"So can I go?" asked Bella.

"You can go if you let me come too," said her dad.

B. Check for the appropriate use of quotation marks in the dialogue.

Ms. Hooper and Kafi: Corrections

A. Correct use of quotation marks is shown below.

"Kafi, please stop talking. The class is working

quietly right now," said Ms. Hooper.

"It's not me, it's my mouth," said Kafi.

"Please control your mouth," said Ms. Hooper.

"I've tried, but it runs away from me all the time,"

said Kafi.

"It must be must be tired, then," said Ms. Hooper.

"Maybe it needs a rest," said Kafi.

B. Check for the appropriate use of quotation marks in the dialogue.

Cool Animal Moves: Corrections

A. **Words that use apostrophes to show possession are underlined below.**

Not all animals walk or run on the ground.

A kangaroo's back legs are perfect for hopping.

A snake's stomach muscles help it wriggle forward.

A gecko's feet are covered in tiny hairs so that it can stick to ceilings and walk upside down.

B. **Sentences will vary. Check for the correct use of apostrophes.**

1. *Conah's cousin is silly.*

2. *The room's walls are interesting.*

3. *The dog's bed is soft.*

Twins: Corrections

A. **Words that use apostrophes to show possession are underlined below.**

Jane and Bea are twins, but they are very different. Jane's hair is red. Bea's hair is brown. Jane's knees are covered in freckles; Bea's knees have no freckles. Jane loves roller coasters; Bea hates going fast. Jane's laugh is loud. Bea's laugh is so quiet you can hardly hear her laugh.

B. **Sentences will vary. Check for the correct use of apostrophes.**

1. *Anita's goldfish is peaceful.*

2. *The school's baseball team is good.*

3. *The ducks' feet are orange.*

The Terrible Temper: Corrections

A. Words that use apostrophes to show possession are underlined below.

Brenda had a terrible temper. She made faces

when her friend's lunch looked better than hers did.

She stamped her foot when her brother's school

project was more interesting than hers was. Brenda's

parents weren't sure what to do. They'd never seen a

temper as terrible as Brenda's temper.

B. Sentences will vary. Check for the correct use of apostrophes.

1. The bears' fur is soft.

2. The roses' petals are red.

3. Camille's bed is lumpy.

Insects: Corrections

A. Words that use apostrophes to show possession are underlined below.

Insects protect themselves in interesting ways. A

butterfly's colorful wings and a bee's yellow stripes

tell others that they taste bad! A moth's brown wings

keep it hidden on a tree's bark. A ladybird's smell

keeps others away.

B. Sentences will vary. Check for the correct use of apostrophes.

1. Ramona's hamster is grumpy.

2. Belinda's necklace is sparkly.

3. The swimmers' team is speedy.

Small Towns: Corrections

A. Proper nouns are underlined.

Many small towns have interesting things to see. Some towns have big sculptures made of wood and plastic. The World's Largest Crayon is in Easton, Pennsylvania. It was built in October 2003. The Giant Coffee Pot is in Winston, North Carolina. There's a giant peanut in Ashburn, Georgia and a huge egg in Winlock, Washington.

B. Types of proper nouns in the passage are shown below.

- *names of places*
- *months of the year*
- *names given to specific things*

- *names of cities and towns*
- *names of states*

C. Check for appropriate examples of proper nouns.

Arbor Day: Corrections

A. Proper nouns are underlined.

Arbor is another word for "tree." Arbor Day is a day when people plant trees. This is how Arbor Day started. In 1854, a man named J. Sterling Morton went to the Great Plains in Nebraska. The Great Plains had no trees. There was no shade from the sun. Morton created Arbor Day. The first Arbor Day was Friday, April 10, 1874.

B. Types of proper nouns in the passage are shown below.

- *days of the week*
- *names of people*
- *months of the year*

- *name of special events*
- *names of places*
- *names of states*

C. Check for appropriate examples of proper nouns.

First Person in Space: Corrections

A. **Proper nouns are underlined.**

In 1961, a man named Yuri Gagarin became

the first person in space. His spaceship was called

Vostok 1. On Wednesday, April 12, 1961, he made

one full circle around Earth. When he landed, he

was famous.

B. **Types of proper nouns in the passage are shown below.**

- day of the week   - months of the year
- names of people   - names given to
- names of places   specific things (spaceship)

C. **Check for appropriate examples of proper nouns.**

Hull House: Corrections

A. **Proper nouns are underlined.**

In the 1800s, there were many poor people in

Chicago, Illinois. A woman named Jane Addams

wanted to help the poor. Jane Addams and her friend

Ellen Gates Star had an idea. They started a club

where people could come and learn new skills. The

club was called Hull House. They helped a lot of

people at Hull House.

B. **Types of proper nouns in the passage are shown below.**

- names of people   - names of cities and towns
- names of states   - names of places

C. **Check for appropriate examples of proper nouns.**

Ring the Bell: Corrections

A. The alphabetized list and riddle answer are given below.

pears	1.	l	a	d̲	l	e
quill	2.	l	o̲	o	s	e
louse	3.	l	o̲	u	s	e
probe	4.	p	e	a	r̲	s
ladle	5.	p	r	o	b̲	e
loose	6.	q	u	e̲	s	t
rolls	7.	q	u	i	l̲	l
quest	8.	r	o	l̲	l	s

What asks no questions but needs to be answered?

d   o   o   r   b   e   l   l

When the Sun Goes Down: Corrections

A. The alphabetized list and riddle answer are given below.

moose	1.	f	o	u	n	d̲
glare	2.	g	l	a̲	r	e
knock	3.	g	l	o	r̲	y
lemon	4.	k̲	n	e	e	s
mouse	5.	k	n̲	o	c	k
knees	6.	l	e̲	m	o	n
found	7.	m	o	o	s̲	e
glory	8.	m	o	u	s̲	e

The more you have of this, the less you can see. What is it?

d   a   r   k   n   e   s   s

A Room You Can Eat: Corrections

A. The alphabetized list and riddle answer are given below.

moody   **1.** a | m | a z e

lords   **2.** c | u | b b y

girls   **3.** g i r l | s |

murky   **4.** l e e c | h |

cubby   **5.** l | o | o r d s

moldy   **6.** m | o | l d y

amaze   **7.** m o o d y

leech   **8.** m | m | u r k y

What kind of room has no windows or doors?

m u s h r o o m

Being a Writer™ | **63**

The Giant Ant: Corrections

A. The alphabetized list and riddle answer are given below.

maple   **1.** h e d | g | e

sharp   **2.** h o | l | e s

towel   **3.** l | e | v e l

hedge   **4.** m a | p | l e

tense   **5.** s | h | a r k

holes   **6.** s h | a | r p

shark   **7.** t e | n | s e

level   **8.** t | t | o w e l

What is the largest ant in the world?

e l e p h a n t

64 | Being a Writer™

Football: Corrections

A. Corrections are given below.

Football is a team sport. That means that

all the *player* on a team work together to help

players

their

there team win. Some players try to score points by

They kick

making a touchdown. Kick, throw, or run with the

ball. Some players try to stop the other team from

making a touchdown. They tackle the player with

the ball. Football can be a fun sport to watch.

B. **Check for the appropriate use of practiced skills in the passage.**

At the Mall: Corrections

A. Corrections are given below.

has

The mall is a scary place. Each floor have

person

hundreds of people. Every people is a stranger.

J

The scariest day of my life was the day my sister

justine took me there. She went into a clothes shop.

Suddenly she disappeared. I saw lots of shirts, dresses,

pants   J

and, But justine was gone!

B. **Check for the appropriate use of practiced skills in the passage.**

A Caterpillar: Corrections

A.   Corrections are given below.

A caterpillar has many ~~leg~~ *legs*. It can crawl but it

can't fly. A caterpillar builds a soft shell around

itself. The shell protects ~~them~~ *it* from the wind and

rain. Day⊙week⊙and months pass. The caterpillar

changes. When it finally leaves its shell,

it ~~are~~ *is* a butterfly. Now it can fly!

B.   Check for the appropriate use of practiced skills in the passage.

Travel: Corrections

A.   Corrections are given below.

I want to travel to new places. On my world map,

I ~~draws~~ *draw* a circle around egypt⊙Spain⊙and Timbuktu.

These are the places I want to go to first.

I want to travel to big cities and small towns.

I want to ride on planes⊙on trains⊙and in boats.

I know the people I meet won't all speak English.

But they will see how happy I ~~is~~ *am* to meet them.

B.   Check for the appropriate use of practiced skills in the passage.

Being a Writer.
Reorder Information

Kindergarten

Complete Classroom Package   BW-CPK

Contents: Teacher's Manual (2 volumes) and 19 trade books.

Available separately

Teacher's Manual, vol. 1	BW-TMK-V1
Teacher's Manual, vol. 2	BW-TMK-V2
Trade book set (19 books)	BW-TBSK

Grade 1

Complete Classroom Package   BW-CP1

Contents: Teacher's Manual (2 volumes), Assessment Resource Book, and 21 trade books.

Available separately

Teacher's Manual, vol. 1	BW-TM1-V1
Teacher's Manual, vol. 2	BW-TM1-V2
Assessment Resource Book	BW-AB1
CD-ROM Grade 1 Reproducible Materials	BW-CDR1
Trade book set (21 books)	BW-TBS1

Grade 2

Complete Classroom Package   BW-CP2

Contents: Teacher's Manual (2 volumes), Skill Practice Teaching Guide, Assessment Resource Book, 25 Student Writing Handbooks, 25 Student Skill Practice Books, and 27 trade books.

Available separately

Teacher's Manual, vol. 1	BW-TM2-V1
Teacher's Manual, vol. 2	BW-TM2-V2
Skill Practice Teaching Guide	BW-STG2
Assessment Resource Book	BW-AB2
Student Writing Handbook pack (5 books)	BW-SB2-Q5
Student Skill Practice Book pack (5 books)	BW-SSB2-Q5
CD-ROM Grade 2 Reproducible Materials	BW-CDR2
Trade book set (27 books)	BW-TBS2

Grade 3

Complete Classroom Package   BW-CP3

Contents: Teacher's Manual (2 volumes), Skill Practice Teaching Guide, Assessment Resource Book, 25 Student Writing Handbooks, 25 Student Skill Practice Books, and 31 trade books.

Available separately

Teacher's Manual, vol. 1	BW-TM3-V1
Teacher's Manual, vol. 2	BW-TM3-V2
Skill Practice Teaching Guide	BW-STG3
Assessment Resource Book	BW-AB3
Student Writing Handbook pack (5 books)	BW-SB3-Q5
Student Skill Practice Book pack (5 books)	BW-SSB3-Q5
CD-ROM Grade 3 Reproducible Materials	BW-CDR3
Trade book set (31 books)	BW-TBS3

Grade 4

Complete Classroom Package   BW-CP4

Contents: Teacher's Manual (2 volumes), Skill Practice Teaching Guide, Assessment Resource Book, 30 Student Writing Handbooks, 30 Student Skill Practice Books, and 25 trade books.

Available separately

Teacher's Manual, vol. 1	BW-TM4-V1
Teacher's Manual, vol. 2	BW-TM4-V2
Skill Practice Teaching Guide	BW-STG4
Assessment Resource Book	BW-AB4
Student Writing Handbook pack (5 books)	BW-SB4-Q5
Student Skill Practice Book pack (5 books)	BW-SSB4-Q5
CD-ROM Grade 4 Reproducible Materials	BW-CDR4
Trade book set (25 books)	BW-TBS4

Grade 5

Complete Classroom Package   BW-CP5

Contents: Teacher's Manual (2 volumes), Skill Practice Teaching Guide, Assessment Resource Book, 30 Student Writing Handbooks, 30 Student Skill Practice Books, and 25 trade books.

Available separately

Teacher's Manual, vol. 1	BW-TM5-V1
Teacher's Manual, vol. 2	BW-TM5-V2
Skill Practice Teaching Guide	BW-STG5
Assessment Resource Book	BW-AB5
Student Writing Handbook pack (5 books)	BW-SB5-Q5
Student Skill Practice Book pack (5 books)	BW-SSB5-Q5
CD-ROM Grade 5 Reproducible Materials	BW-CDR5
Trade book set (25 books)	BW-TBS5

Ordering Information:

To order call 800.666.7270 * fax 510.842.0348 * log on to www.devstu.org * e-mail pubs@devstu.org

Or Mail Your Order to:

Developmental Studies Center * Publications Department * 2000 Embarcadero, Suite 305 * Oakland, CA 94606-5300

DEVELOPMENTAL STUDIES CENTER.